Zoom In on
Rocks and Minerals

Ores

Andrea Rivera

abdopublishing.com

Published by Abdo Zoom™, PO Box 398166, Minneapolis, Minnesota 55439. Copyright © 2018 by Abdo Consulting Group, Inc. International copyrights reserved in all countries. No part of this book may be reproduced in any form without written permission from the publisher. Abdo Zoom™ is a trademark and logo of Abdo Consulting Group, Inc.

Printed in the United States of America, North Mankato, Minnesota
032017
092017

 **THIS BOOK CONTAINS RECYCLED MATERIALS**

Cover Photo: Andriy Solovyov/Shutterstock Images
Interior Photos: Andriy Solovyov/Shutterstock Images, 1; Shutterstock Images, 5, 7, 8–9, 9, 10, 11, 15, 17, 19, 21; Henri Koskinen/Shutterstock Images, 6; Kotomiti Okuma/Shutterstock Images, 12–13; Marina Zezelina/Shutterstock Images, 13; iStockphoto, 14; Andrey N. Bannov/Shutterstock Images, 16; John Brueske/Shutterstock Images, 18

Editor: Emily Temple
Series Designer: Madeline Berger
Art Direction: Dorothy Toth

Publisher's Cataloging-in-Publication Data
Names: Rivera, Andrea, author.
Title: Ores / by Andrea Rivera.
Description: Minneapolis, MN : Abdo Zoom, 2018. | Series: Rocks and minerals | Includes bibliographical references and index.
Identifiers: LCCN 2017930294 | ISBN 9781532120466 (lib. bdg.) | ISBN 9781614797579 (ebook) | ISBN 9781614798132 (Read-to-me ebook)
Subjects: LCSH: Ores--Juvenile literature. | Mineralogy--Juvenile literature.
Classification: DDC 553--dc23
LC record available at http://lccn.loc.gov/2017930294

Table of Contents

Science

Ores are rocks that
have metal inside them.
Ores form from **minerals**.
They are found in nature.

Metals from ores are shiny.
They can be shaped easily.

They can also conduct
heat and electricity.

Technology

Ores are found in rocks. People **mine** the ores. Some ores are found near the surface. The rocks are blasted away.

Other ores are underground. Machines dig tunnels so people can get to them.

Next, trucks move the rocks with ores. The rocks are crushed. Then the ores are removed.

Some ores are removed using water. Others are melted away from rock.

Engineering

People use metals from ores every day. Aluminum is used often. It is light.

Soda cans are made from aluminum. So are airplanes.

Iron comes from iron ore. It is strong.

Iron is used to make steel. Many tall buildings are made using steel.

Metals from ores are used in jewelry. Sterling silver and gold are common. These can be melted and poured into a mold.

They can also be stretched and hammered to make jewelry.

Math

Coins can be made of metals. A United States penny is made of copper and zinc. It is one cent.

Nickels are five cents. Dimes are ten cents.

nickel

dime

They are both made of nickel and copper.

19

- Gold comes from ore. The largest gold statue in the world is of Buddha. It is 9.8 feet (3 m) tall. It weighs 5.5 tons (5,000 kg).

- There are 147.3 million ounces (4.2 million kg) of gold in the US Depository at Fort Knox in Kentucky.

- The world's deepest mines are in South Africa. Much of the gold mined in the world comes from there.

Glossary

conduct - to allow electricity or heat to move through something.

electricity - a form of energy that can be carried through wires.

mine - to dig in earth for metal or minerals.

mineral - a substance that forms naturally under the ground.

sterling silver - silver mixed with other metals so that it is stronger.

Booklinks

For more information on ores, please visit abdobooklinks.com

Learn even more with the Abdo Zoom STEAM database. Check out abdozoom.com for more information.

Index